THE LOVE OF THE NIGHTINGALE

by
Timberlake Wertenbaker

The Dramatic Publishing Company
Woodstock, Illinois • London, England • Melbourne, Australia

For Kate

Listen. This is the noise of myth. It makes the same
  sound as shadow. Can you hear it?

Eavan Boland, *The Journey*

Now, by myself, I am nothing; yea, full oft
I have regarded woman's fortunes thus,
That we are nothing; who in our fathers' house
Live, I suppose, the happiest, while young,
Of all mankind; for ever pleasantly
Does Folly nurture all. Then, when we come
To full discretion and maturity,
We are thrust out and marketed abroad,
Far from our parents and ancestral gods,
Some to strange husbands, some to barbarous,
One to a rude, one to a wrangling home;
And these, after the yoking of a night,
We are bound to like, and deem it well with us.

                    Much
I envy thee thy life: and most of all,
That thou hast never had experience
Of a strange land.

Two fragments from Sophocles's lost play, *Tereus*
Translated by Sir George Young

THE LOVE OF THE NIGHTINGALE was first performed by the Royal Shakespeare Company at The Other Place, Stratford-upon-Avon, on 28 October 1988. The cast was as follows:

MALE CHORUS . . . . David Acton, Stephen Gordon, Richard Haddon Haines, Patrick Miller, Edward Rawle-Hicks

FIRST SOLDIER . . . . Patrick Miller
SECOND SOLDIER . . . . David Acton
PROCNE . . . . Marie Mullen
PHILOMELE . . . . Katy Behean
KING PANDION . . . . Richard Haddon Haines
THE QUEEN . . . . Joan Blackham
TEREUS . . . . Peter Lennon

Female Chorus

HERO . . . . Cate Hamer
IRIS . . . . Claudette Williams
JUNE . . . . Joan Blackham
ECHO . . . . Joanna Roth
HELEN . . . . Jill Spurrier

Actors in the Hippolytus play

APHRODITE . . . . Claudette Williams
PHAEDRA . . . . Cate Hamer
THE NURSE . . . . Jill Spurrier
FEMALE CHORUS . . . . Joanna Roth
HIPPOLYTUS . . . . Edward Rawle-Hicks
THESEUS . . . . David Acton
MALE CHORUS . . . . Stephen Gordon

THE CAPTAIN . . . . Tony Armatrading
NIOBE . . . . Jenni George
SERVANT . . . . Joanna Roth
ITYS . . . . Nicholas Besley/Alexander Knott

Director	Garry Hynes
Lighting	Geraint Pughe
Music	Ilona Sekacz

THE LOVE OF THE NIGHTINGALE

A Full Length Play
For Seven Men and Seven Women, and Two Choruses*

CHARACTERS

MALE CHORUS
FIRST SOLDIER
SECOND SOLDIER
PROCNE
PHILOMELE
KING PANDION
THE QUEEN
TEREUS
HERO
IRIS
JUNE — Female Chorus
ECHO
HELEN
APHRODITE
PHAEDRA
THE NURSE
FEMALE CHORUS — Actors in the Hippolytus play
HIPPOLYTUS
THESEUS
MALE CHORUS
THE CAPTAIN
NIOBE
SERVANT
ITYS

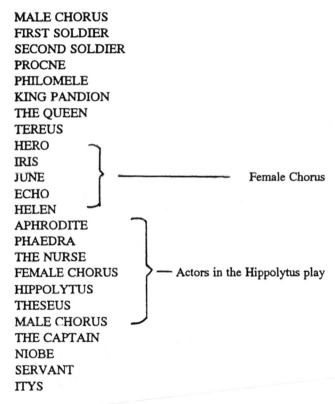

*The Chorus never speak together, except the one time it
  is specifically indicated in the text.

THE LOVE OF THE NIGHTINGALE

SCENE ONE

Athens. The MALE CHORUS.

MALE CHORUS. War.

(Two SOLDIERS come on, with swords and shields.)

FIRST SOLDIER. You cur!
SECOND SOLDIER. You cat's whisker.
FIRST SOLDIER. You flea's foot.
SECOND SOLDIER. You particle.
  (Pause.)
  You son of a bitch.
FIRST SOLDIER. You son of a lame hyena.
SECOND SOLDIER. You son of a bleeding whore.
FIRST SOLDIER. You son of a woman!
  (Pause.)
  I'll slice your drooping genitalia.
SECOND SOLDIER. I'll pierce your windy asshole.
FIRST SOLDIER. I'll drink from your skull.
  (Pause.)
  Coward!
SECOND SOLDIER. Braggard.
FIRST SOLDIER. You worm.
SECOND SOLDIER. You—man.
  (They fight.)

9

MALE CHORUS. And now, death.
(The FIRST SOLDIER kills the SECOND SOLDIER.)
SECOND SOLDIER. Murderer!
FIRST SOLDIER. Corpse!
MALE CHORUS. We begin here because no life ever has been untouched by war.
MALE CHORUS. Everyone loves to discuss war.
MALE CHORUS. And yet its outcome, death, is shrouded in silence.
MALE CHORUS. Wars make death acceptable. The gods are less cruel if it is man's fault.
MALE CHORUS. Perhaps, but this is not our story. War is the inevitable background, the ruins of the distance establishing place and perspective.
MALE CHORUS. Athens is at war, but in the palace of the Athenian king Pandion, two sisters discuss life's charms and the attractions of men.

SCENE TWO

PROCNE, PHILOMELE.

PROCNE. Don't say that, Philomele.
PHILOMELE. It's the truth: he's so handsome I want to wrap my legs around him.
PROCNE. That's not how it's done.
PHILOMELE. How can I know if no one will tell me? Look at the sweat shining down his body. My feet will curl around the muscles of his back. How is it done, Procne, tell me, please? If you don't tell me, I'll ask Niobe and she'll tell me all wrong.

PROCNE. I'll tell you if you tell me something.

PHILOMELE. I'll tell you everything I know, sweet sister. *(Pause.)* I don't know anything.

PROCNE. You know yourself.

PHILOMELE. Oh, yes, I feel such things, Procne, such things. Tigers, rivers, serpents, here, in my stomach, a little below. I'll tell you how the serpent uncurls inside me if you tell me how it's done.

PROCNE. That's not what I meant, Philomele, I'm going to marry soon.

PHILOMELE. I envy you, sister, you'll know everything then. What are they like? Men?

PROCNE. Look: they fight.

PHILOMELE. What are they like: naked?

PROCNE. Spongy.

PHILOMELE. What?

PROCNE. I haven't seen one yet, but that's what they told me to prepare me. They have sponges.

PHILOMELE. Where?

PROCNE. Here. Getting bigger and smaller and moving up and down. I didn't listen very carefully, I'll know soon enough. Philomele, when I am married, will you want to come and visit me?

PHILOMELE. Yes, sister, yes. I'll visit you every day and you'll let me watch.

PROCNE. Philomele! Can't you think of anything else?

PHILOMELE. Not today. Tomorrow I'll think about wisdom. It must be so beautiful. Warm ripples of light.

PROCNE. I think most of it you can do on your own. The sponge. I think it detaches.

PHILOMELE. I wouldn't want to do it on my own. I want to run my hands down bronzed skin. Ah, I can feel the tiger again.

PROCNE. If I went far away, would you still want to come and visit me?

PHILOMELE. I will cross any sea to visit you and your handsome husband, sister. *(Pause.)* When I'm old enough, I won't stop doing it, whatever it is. Life must be so beautiful when you're older. It's beautiful now. Sometimes I'm so happy.

PROCNE. Quiet, Philomele! Never say you're happy. It wakes up the gods and then they look at you and that is never a good thing. Take it back, now.

PHILOMELE. You taught me not to lie, sister.

PROCNE. I wish I didn't have to leave home. I worry about you.

PHILOMELE. Life is sweet, my sister, and I love everything in it. The feelings. Athens. You. And that brave young warrior fighting to protect us. Oh!

PROCNE. Philomele? Ah.

He's dead.

PHILOMELE. Crumpled. Procne, was it my fault? Should I have held my tongue?

PROCNE. Athens is at war, men must die.

PHILOMELE. I'm frightened. I don't want to leave this room ever.

PROCNE. You must try to become more moderate. Measure in all things, remember, it's what the philosophers recommend.

PHILOMELE. Will the philosophers start speaking again after the war? Procne, can we go and listen to them?

PROCNE. I won't be here.

PHILOMELE. Procne, don't go.

PROCNE. It's our parents' will. They know best.

(Pause.)

You will come to me if I ask for you, you will?

PHILOMELE. Yes.

PROCNE. I want you to promise. Remember you must never break a promise.

PHILOMELE. I promise. I will want to. I promise again.

PROCNE. That makes me happy. Ah.

SCENE THREE

The palace of King Pandion. KING PANDION, the QUEEN, TEREUS, PROCNE, PHILOMELE, the MALE CHORUS.

MALE CHORUS. Athens won the war with the help of an ally from the north.

MALE CHORUS. The leader of the liberators was called Tereus.

KING PANDION. No liberated country is ungrateful. That is a rule. You will take what you want from our country. It will be given with gratitude. We are ready.

TEREUS. I came not out of greed but in the cause of justice, King Pandion. But I have come to love this country and its inhabitants.

QUEEN *(to KING PANDION)*. He wants to stay! I knew it! *(Pause.)*

KING PANDION. Of course if you wish to stay in Athens that is your right. We can only remind you this is a small city. But you must stay if you wish.

TEREUS. No. I must go back north. There has been trouble while I've conducted this war. What I want—is to bring some of your country to mine, its manners, its ease, its civilized discourse.

QUEEN (to KING PANDION). I knew it: he wants Procne.

KING PANDION. I can send you some of our tutors. The philosophers, I'm afraid, are rather independent.

TEREUS. I have always believed that culture was kept by the women.

KING PANDION. Ours are not encouraged to go abroad.

TEREUS. But they have a reputation for wisdom. Is that false?

QUEEN. Be careful, he's crafty.

KING PANDION. It is true. Our women are the best.

TEREUS. So.

QUEEN. I knew it.

(Pause.)

KING PANDION. She's yours, Tereus. Procne—

PROCNE. But, Father—

KING PANDION. Your husband.

PROCNE. Mother—

QUEEN. What can I say?

KING PANDION. I am only sad you will live so far away.

PHILOMELE. Can I go with her?

QUEEN. Quiet, child.

TEREUS (to PROCNE). I will love and respect you.

MALE CHORUS. It didn't happen that quickly. It took months and much indirect discourse. But that is the gist of it. The end was known from the beginning.

MALE CHORUS. After an elaborate wedding in which King Pandion solemnly gave his daughter to the hero, Tereus, the two left for Thrace. There was relief in Athens. His army had become expensive, rude, rowdy.

MALE CHORUS. Had always been, but we see things differently in peace. That is why peace is so painful.

MALE CHORUS. Nothing to blur the waters. We look down to the bottom.

MALE CHORUS. And on a clear day, we see our own reflections.

(Pause.)

MALE CHORUS. In due course, Procne had a child, a boy called Itys. Five years passed.

SCENE FOUR

PROCNE and her companions, the FEMALE CHORUS: HERO, ECHO, IRIS, JUNE, HELEN.

PROCNE. Where have all the words gone?

HERO. She sits alone, hour after hour, turns her head away and laments.

IRIS. We don't know how to act, we don't know what to say.

HERO. She turns from us in grief.

JUNE. Boredom.

ECHO. Homesick.

HERO. It is difficult to come to a strange land.

HELEN. You will always be a guest there, never call it your own, never rest in the kindness of history.

ECHO. Your story intermingled with events, no. You will be outside.

IRIS. And if it is the land of your husband can you even say you have chosen it?

JUNE. She is not one of us.

HERO. A shared childhood makes friends between women.

ECHO. The places we walked together, our first smells.

HELEN. But an unhappy woman can do much harm. She has already dampened our play.

JUNE. Mocked the occupation of our hours, scorned.

IRIS. What shall we do?

HELEN. I fear the future.

PROCNE. Where have the words gone?

ECHO. Gone, Procne, the words?

PROCNE. There were so many. Everything that was, had a word and every word was something. None of these meanings half in the shade, unclear.

IRIS. We speak the same language, Procne.

PROCNE. The words are the same, but point to different things. We aspire to clarity in sound, you like the silences in between.

HERO. We offered to initiate you.

PROCNE. Barbarian practices. I am an Athenian: I know the truth is found by logic and happiness lies in the truth.

HERO. Truth is full of darkness.

PROCNE. No, truth is good and beautiful. See...*(Pause.)* I must have someone to talk to.

JUNE. We've tried. See...

HERO. She turns away.

PROCNE. How we talked. Our words played, caressed each other, our words were tossed lightly, a challenge to catch. Where is she now? Who shares those games with her? Or is she silent too?

ECHO. Silent, Procne, who?

PROCNE. My sister. *(Pause.)* My friend. I want to talk to her. I want her here.

HERO. You have a family, Procne, a husband, a child.

PROCNE. I cannot talk to my husband. I have nothing to say to my son. I want her here. She must come here.

HELEN. It's a long way and a dangerous one for a young girl. Let her be, Procne.

PROCNE. I want my sister here.

HELEN. She could come to harm.

PROCNE. Tereus could bring her, she'll be safe with him.

ECHO. Tereus.

HELEN. Dangers on the sea, he won't want you to risk them.

PROCNE. He can go alone. I'll wait here and look after the country.

ECHO. Tereus.

HERO. Will your sister want to come to a strange land?

PROCNE. She will want what I want.

HELEN. Don't ask her to come, Procne.

PROCNE. Why not?

HERO. This is no country for a strange young girl.

PROCNE. She will be with me.

HERO. She won't listen.

HELEN. I am worried. It is not something I can say. There are no words for forebodings.

HERO. We are only brushed by possibilities.

ECHO. A beating of wings.

JUNE. Best to say nothing. Procne? May we go now?

PROCNE. To your rituals?

JUNE. Yes, it's time.

PROCNE. Very well, go.

   (They go.)

   This silence...this silence...

SCENE FIVE

The theatre in Athens. KING PANDION, TEREUS, HIP-POLYTUS, THESEUS.

KING PANDION. Procne has always been so sensible.
Why, suddenly, does she ask for her sister?

TEREUS. She didn't explain. She insisted I come to you
and I did what she asked.

KING PANDION. I understand, Tereus, but such a long
journey...Procne's not ill?

TEREUS. She was well when I left. She has her child,
companions.

KING PANDION. Philomele is still very young. And yet,
I allowed Procne to go so far away...What do you think,
Tereus?

TEREUS. You're her father.

KING PANDION. And you, her husband.

TEREUS. I only meant Procne would accept any decision
you made. It is a long journey.

(APHRODITE enters.)

APHRODITE. I am Aphrodite, goddess of love, resplen-
dent and mighty, revered on earth, courted in heaven,
all pay tribute to my fearful power.

KING PANDION. Do you know this play, Tereus?

TEREUS. No.

KING PANDION. I find plays help me think. You catch a
phrase, recognize a character. Perhaps this play will
help us come to a decision.

APHRODITE. I honour those who kneel before me, but
that proud heart which dares defy me, that haughty
heart I bring low.

TEREUS. That's sound.

KING PANDION. Do you have good theatre in Thrace?

TEREUS. We prefer sport.

KING PANDION. Then you are like Hippolytus.

TEREUS. Who?

KING PANDION. Listen.

APHRODITE. Hippolytus turns his head away. Hippolytus prefers the hard chase to the soft bed, wild game to foreplay, but chaste Hippolytus shall be crushed this very day.

(APHRODITE exits. The QUEEN and PHILOMELE enter.)

PHILOMELE. We're late! I've missed Aphrodite.

KING PANDION. She only told us it was going to end badly, but we already know that. It's a tragedy.

(Enter PHAEDRA.)

QUEEN. There's Phaedra. *(To TEREUS.)* Phaedra is married to Theseus, The King of Athens. Hippolytus is Theseus' son by his previous mistress, the Amazon Queen, who's now dead, and so Phaedra's stepson. Phaedra has three children of her own.

PHAEDRA. Hold me, hold me, hold up my head. The strength of my limbs is melting away.

PHILOMELE. How beautiful to love like that! "The strength of my limbs is melting away." Is that what you feel for Procne, Tereus?

QUEEN. Philomele! *(To TEREUS.)* Phaedra's fallen in love with Hippolytus.

TEREUS. Her own stepson! That's wrong.

KING PANDION. That's what makes it a tragedy. When you love the right person it's a comedy.

PHAEDRA. Oh, pity me, pity me, what have I done? What will become of me? I have strayed from the path of good sense.

TEREUS. Why should we pity her? These plays condone vice.

KING PANDION. Perhaps they only show us the uncomfortable folds of the human heart.

PHAEDRA. I am mad, struck down by the malice of the implacable god.

PHILOMELE. You see, Tereus, love is a god and you cannot control him.

QUEEN. Here's the nurse. She always gives good advice.

(The NURSE enters.)

NURSE. So: you love. You are not the first nor the last. You want to kill yourself? Must all who love die? No, Phaedra, the god has stricken you, how dare you rebel? Be bold, and love. That is god's will.

TEREUS. Terrible advice.

PHILOMELE. No, Tereus, you must obey the gods. Are you blasphemous up there in Thrace?

KING PANDION. Philomele, you are talking to a king.

TEREUS. And to a brother, let her speak, Pandion.

NURSE. I have a remedy. Trust me.

KING PANDION. Procne has asked for you. She wants you to go back with Tereus to Thrace.

PHILOMELE. To Thrace? To Procne? Oh, yes.

KING PANDION. You want to leave your parents? Athens?

PHILOMELE. I promised Procne I would go if she ever asked for me.

KING PANDION. You were a child.

TEREUS. We have no theatre or even philosophers in Thrace, Philomele.

PHILOMELE. I have to keep my word.

TEREUS. Why?

PHILOMELE. Because that is honourable, Tereus.

QUEEN. Listen to the chorus. The playwright always speaks through the chorus.

FEMALE CHORUS. Love, stealing with grace into the heart you wish to destroy, love, turning us blind with the bitter poison of desire, love, come not my way. And when you whirl through the streets, wild steps to unchained rhythms, love, I pray you, brush not against me, love, I beg you, pass me by.

TEREUS. Ah!

PHILOMELE. I would never say that, would you, brother Tereus? I want to feel everything there is to feel. Don't you?

TEREUS. No!

KING PANDION. Tereus, what's the matter?

TEREUS. Nothing. The heat.

PHAEDRA. Oh, I am destroyed forever.

PHILOMELE. Poor Phaedra.

TEREUS. You pity her, Philomele?

QUEEN. Hippolytus has just heard in what way Phaedra loves him. He's furious.

HIPPOLYTUS. Woman, counterfeit coin, why did the gods put you in the world? If we must have sons, let us buy them in the temples and bypass the concourse of these noxious women. I hate you women, hate, hate and hate you.

PHILOMELE. This is horrible. It's not Phaedra's fault she loves him.

TEREUS. She could keep silent about it.

PHILOMELE. When you love you want to imprison the one you love in your words, in your tenderness.

TEREUS. How do you know all this, Philomele?

PHILOMELE. Sometimes I feel the whole world beating inside me.

TEREUS. Philomele...

(PHAEDRA screams offstage, then staggers on.)

QUEEN. Phaedra's killed herself and there's Theseus just back from his travels.

THESEUS. My wife! What have I said or done to drive you to this horrible death? She calls me to her, she can still speak. What prayers, what orders, what entreaties do you leave your grieving husband? Oh, my poor love, speak! *(He listens.)* Hippolytus! Has dared to rape my wife!

TEREUS. Phaedra has lied! That's vile.

PHILOMELE. Why destroy what you love? It's the god.

THESEUS. Father Poseidon, great and ancient sea-god, you once allotted me three wishes. With one of these, I pray you now, kill my son.

QUEEN. That happens offstage. A giant wave comes out of the sea and crashes Hippolytus's chariot against the rocks. Here's the male chorus.

MALE CHORUS. Sometimes I believe in a kind power, wise and all-knowing but when I see the acts of men and their destinies, my hopes grow dim. Fortune twists and turns and life is endless wandering.

KING PANDION. The play's coming to an end, and I still haven't reached a decision. Queen...

MALE CHORUS. What I want from life is to be ordinary.

PHILOMELE. How boring.

QUEEN. Hippolytus has come back to Athens to die. He's
wounded. The head.

FEMALE CHORUS. Poor Hippolytus, I weep at your piti-
ful fate. And I rage against the gods who sent you far
away, out of your father's lands to meet with such di-
saster from the sea-god's wave.

KING PANDION. That's the phrase. Philomele, you must
not leave your father's lands. You'll stay here.

PHILOMELE. But, Father, I'm not Hippolytus. You
haven't cursed me. And Tereus isn't Phaedra, look.
(She laughs.)

TEREUS. I have expert sailors, I don't think we'll crash
against the rocks.

KING PANDION. It's such a long journey.

TEREUS. We'll travel swiftly. Procne is so impatient to
see her sister. We must go soon, or she'll fall ill with
worry.

KING PANDION. When?

TEREUS. Tomorrow.

HIPPOLYTUS. Weep for me, weep for me, destroyed,
mangled, trampled underfoot by man and god both un-
just, weep, weep for my death.

PHILOMELE. Ah.

TEREUS. You're crying, Philomele.

PHILOMELE. I felt, I felt—the beating of wings...

KING PANDION. You do not have to go.

PHILOMELE. It's the play, I am so sorry for them all. I
have to go. My promise...

KING PANDION *(to QUEEN)*. It's only a visit, Philomele
will come back to us.

QUEEN. Where is she going?

KING PANDION. To Thrace! Weren't you listening?

MALE and FEMALE CHORUS (*together*). These sorrows have fallen upon us unforeseen.

MALE CHORUS. Fate is irresistible.

FEMALE CHORUS. And there is no escape.

KING PANDION. And now we must applaud the actors.

SCENE SIX

A small ship, sailing north. The MALE CHORUS, PHIL-OMELE, TEREUS, the CAPTAIN.

MALE CHORUS. The journey north:
Row gently out of Piraeus on a starlit night. Sail around Cape Sounion with a good wind, over to Kea for water and provisions. Kea to Andros, a quiet sea. Up the coast of Euboea to the Sporades: Skiathos, Paparethos, Gioura, Pathoura. Skirt the three-fingered promontory of the mainland: Kassandra, Sithounia and Athos of the wild men and into the Thracian sea. The dawns, so loved by the poets.

MALE CHORUS. Rosy fingered, female.

MALE CHORUS. The dawns get colder and colder as we sail north.

(*Pause.*)

MALE CHORUS. Philomele wonders at the beauty of the sea.

MALE CHORUS. Tereus wonders at Philomele's beauty.

MALE CHORUS. We say nothing. And when the order comes.

MALE CHORUS. Such an order.

MALE CHORUS. Six Athenian solders have been sent to accompany Philomele. They stand on the deck, watching. On a dark night, they disappear.
(Pause.)

MALE CHORUS. In the cold dawns, Tereus burns.

MALE CHORUS. Does Philomele know? Ought we to tell her? We are here only to observe, journalists of an antique world, putting horror into words, unable to stop the events we will soon record.

MALE CHORUS. And so we reach the lonely port of Imeros. It is dark, there is no welcome.

MALE CHORUS. We are not expected.

MALE CHORUS. No moon in the sky.

MALE CHORUS. This is unpropitious.

MALE CHORUS. But that we already knew. Could we have done something? And now?

MALE CHORUS. We choose to be accurate, and we record:

SCENE SEVEN

The CAPTAIN, PHILOMELE, NIOBE.

PHILOMELE. Where are we now, Captain?

CAPTAIN. Far north of Athens, miss.

PHILOMELE. I know that, Captain. How far are we from Thrace?

CAPTAIN. A few days, perhaps more. It depends.

PHILOMELE. On you?

CAPTAIN. No. On the sea.

PHILOMELE. Isn't that a fire over there?

CAPTAIN. Yes.

PHILOMELE. That means we're not far from the coast, doesn't it?

CAPTAIN. Yes, it does.

PHILOMELE. Look how high the fire is. It must be a mountain, Captain.

CAPTAIN. Yes, it is.

PHILOMELE. What is it called, Captain, what is it like? I would like to know about all these lands. You must tell me.

CAPTAIN. That would be Mount Athos, miss.

PHILOMELE. Why don't we anchor there, Captain, and climb the mountain.

CAPTAIN. You wouldn't want to go there, miss.

PHILOMELE. Why not, is it ugly?

CAPTAIN. No, but wild men live there, very wild. They kill all women, even female animals are not allowed on that mountain.

PHILOMELE. Why not?

CAPTAIN. They worship male gods. They believe all harm in the world comes from women.

PHILOMELE. Why do they believe that? *(Pause.)* You don't agree with them, do you, Captain?

CAPTAIN. I don't know, miss.

PHILOMELE. If you don't disagree, you agree with them, Captain, that's logic.

CAPTAIN. Women are beautiful.

PHILOMELE. But surely you believe that beauty is truth and goodness as well?

CAPTAIN. That I don't know. I would have to think about it.

PHILOMELE. I'll prove it to you now, I once heard a philosopher do it. I will begin by asking you a lot of questions. You answer yes or no. But you must pay attention. Are you ready?

CAPTAIN. I think so.

PHILOMELE. And when I've proved all this, Captain, you will have to renounce the beliefs of those wild men.

CAPTAIN. I might.

PHILOMELE. You have to promise.

(TEREUS enters.)

TEREUS. Why are the sails up, Captain?

CAPTAIN. We have a good wind, Tereus.

TEREUS. Take them down.

CAPTAIN. We could be becalmed further north and then my men will have to row. They're tired, Tereus.

TEREUS. We're sailing too fast, it's frightening Philomele.

PHILOMELE. I love to feel the wind, Tereus.

TEREUS. Why aren't you asleep?

PHILOMELE. It's such a beautiful night. I was watching the fires on Athos.

TEREUS. Athos? Yes, the hooded men.

PHILOMELE. The Captain was telling me about them.

TEREUS. Lower the sails, Captain.

CAPTAIN. But Tereus—

TEREUS. This isn't a battle, we have time.

(Exit the CAPTAIN.)

NIOBE. I'll take Philomele down with me, my lord.

TEREUS. Not yet.

(Pause.)

Come and talk to me, Philomele.

NIOBE. Entertain his lordship, Philomele.

(Silence.)

TEREUS. Well. You were talking easily enough when I came above.

PHILOMELE. Tell me about my sister, Tereus.

TEREUS. I've already told you.

PHILOMELE. Tell me more. How does she occupy her time?

TEREUS. I don't know. She has women with her.

PHILOMELE. What do they talk about?

TEREUS. What women talk about. I didn't ask you to grill me, Philomele. Talk to me. Talk to me about the night.

PHILOMELE. The night?

(Pause.)

TEREUS. The night. Something! What were you saying to the captain?

PHILOMELE. I was asking him questions, Tereus.

(Silence. The SAILORS sing a song, softly.)

How well they sing.

(Pause.)

TEREUS. Do you want to be married, Philomele?

NIOBE. Oh, yes, my lord. Every young girl wants to be married. Don't you, Philomele?

PHILOMELE. Niobe, go to bed, please.

NIOBE. No, I can't. I mustn't. I will stay here. I must.

PHILOMELE. Why?

NIOBE. It wouldn't be right...A young girl. A man.

PHILOMELE. I am with my brother, Niobe.

TEREUS. You can go, Niobe.

NIOBE. Yes, yes. Well...I will go and talk to the sailors. Although what they will say to an old woman...no one wants to talk to an old woman. But so it is...I'm not far, I'm not far. The Queen said I was not to go far...

(Pause.)

TEREUS. You're beautiful.

PHILOMELE. Procne always said I was. But the Athenians admired her because of her dignity. Has she kept that in all her years?

TEREUS. In the moonlight, your skin seems transparent.

PHILOMELE. We used to put water out in the full moon and wash our faces in it. We thought it would give us the skin of a goddess. I still do it in memory of my sister. Does she still let out that rhythmical laugh when she thinks you're being foolish? Always on one note, then stopped abruptly. Does she laugh with her women?

TEREUS. I don't know...

PHILOMELE. Does she laugh at you?

TEREUS. Philomele.

PHILOMELE. Yes, brother.

TEREUS. What sort of man do you want to marry? A king?

PHILOMELE. Why not? A great king. Or a prince. Or a noble captain.

TEREUS. Not necessarily from Athens?

PHILOMELE. No. As long as he is wise.

TEREUS. Wise?

PHILOMELE. But then, all kings are wise, aren't they? They have to be or they wouldn't be kings.

TEREUS. You are born a king. Nothing can change that.

PHILOMELE. But you still have to deserve it, don't you?

TEREUS. Would you marry a king from the north? Like your sister? Would you do as your sister in all things?

PHILOMELE. What do you mean? Oh, look, they're making fun of Niobe. Niobe! Here!

NIOBE. They say I would be beautiful if I were young and if I were beautiful then I would be young, no one is kind to an old woman, but I don't mind, I've seen the world. You made his lordship laugh, Philomele, I heard it, that's good. All is well when power smiles, that I know.

TEREUS. Philomele wants to marry a king from the north.

NIOBE. Why, yes, a man as great and brave as you.

PHILOMELE. I am happy for my sister and that is enough for me.

NIOBE. Sisters, sisters...

TEREUS. If Procne were...

NIOBE. I had sisters...

PHILOMELE. Procne.

TEREUS. To become ill...

PHILOMELE. What are you saying, Tereus? Wasn't she well when you left? Why didn't you tell me? Why are we going so slowly? Tell the captain to go faster.

TEREUS. I didn't say that, but if...

NIOBE. Yes, I had many sisters.

TEREUS Things happen.

NIOBE. Too many...

PHILOMELE. My love will protect her, and yours too, Tereus.

TEREUS. Yes...But should...

NIOBE. They died.

PHILOMELE. Niobe!

NIOBE. I only want to to help. I know the world. Old women do. But I'll be quiet now, very quiet.

PHILOMELE. Sister. We will be so happy.

TEREUS. Philomele...

SCENE EIGHT

The MALE CHORUS.

MALE CHORUS. What is a myth? The oblique image of
an unwanted truth, reverberating through time.

MALE CHORUS. And yet, the first, the Greek meaning
of myth, is simply what is delivered by word of mouth,
a myth is speech, public speech.

MALE CHORUS. And myth also means the matter itself,
the content of the speech.

MALE CHORUS. We might ask, has the content become
increasingly unacceptable and therefore the speech more
indirect? How has the meaning of myth been trans-
formed from public speech to an unlikely story? It also
meant counsel, command. Now it is a remote tale.

MALE CHORUS. Let that be, there is no content without
its myth. Fathers and sons, rebellion, collaboration, the
state, every fold and twist of passion, we have uttered
them all. This one, you will say, watching Philomele
watching Tereus watching Philomele, must be about
men and women, yes, you think, a myth for our times,
we understand.

MALE CHORUS. You will be beside the myth. If you
must think of anything, think of countries, silence, but
we cannot rephrase it for you. If we could, why would
we trouble to show you the myth?

MALE CHORUS. We row Philomele north. Does she notice the widening cracks in that fragile edifice, happiness? And what about Procne, the cause perhaps, in any
case the motor of a myth that leaves her mostly absent?

SCENE NINE

PROCNE and the FEMALE CHORUS.

HERO. Sometimes I feel I know things but I cannot prove that I know them or that what I know is true and when I doubt my knowledge it disintegrates into a senseless jumble of possibilities, a puzzle that will not be reassembled, the spider's web in which I lie, immobile, and truth paralysed.

HELEN. Let me put it another way: I have trouble expressing myself. The world I see and the words I have do not match.

JUNE. I am the ugly duckling of fact, so most of the time I try to keep out of the way.

ECHO. Quiet. I shouldn't be here at all.

IRIS. But sometimes it's too much and I must speak. Procne.

PROCNE. What are you women muttering about this time? Something gloomy, no doubt.

IRIS. Procne, we sense danger.

PROCNE. You always sense something, and when I ask you what, you say you don't know, it hasn't happened yet, but it will, or it might. Well, what is it now? What danger? This place is safe. No marauding bands outside, no earthquake, what? What?

HERO. I say danger, she thinks of earthquakes. Doesn't know the first meaning of danger is the power of a lord or master.

HELEN. That one is always in someone's danger.

ECHO. In their power, at their mercy.

JUNE. All service is danger and all marriage too.

IRIS. Procne, listen to me.

PROCNE. What now?

HERO. The sky was so dark this morning...

PROCNE. It'll rain. It always rains.

IRIS. Again.

HERO. I was not talking meteorologically. Images require sympathy.

ECHO. Another way of listening.

IRIS. Procne.

PROCNE. Yes, yes, yes.

HERO. Your sister is on the sea.

PROCNE. She's been on the sea for a month. Have you just found that out?

HELEN. But the sea, the sea...

HERO. And Tereus is a young man.

ECHO. Tereus.

PROCNE. He'll move that much more quickly. Tell me something I don't know.

HERO. When it's too late, it's easy to find the words.

IRIS. Procne.

PROCNE. Leave me alone.

IRIS. If you went down to the seaport. Met them there.

ECHO. A welcome...

PROCNE. I promised Tereus I would stay here and look after his country. I will wait for him here.

IRIS. Procne.

PROCNE. Enough of your nonsense. Be silent.

HELEN. Silent.

ECHO. Silent.

SCENE TEN

*The MALE CHORUS, FIRST SOLDIER, SECOND SOL-
DIER, TEREUS.*

MALE CHORUS. We camp on a desolate beach. Days
   pass.
FIRST SOLDIER. Why are we still here?
SECOND SOLDIER. Tereus has his reasons.
FIRST SOLDIER. I want to go home.
SECOND SOLDIER. We can't until we have the order.
FIRST SOLDIER. It's no more than four days' walk to
   the palace. Why are we still here?
SECOND SOLDIER. I told you: because we haven't been
   ordered to move.
FIRST SOLDIER. Why not?
SECOND SOLDIER. You ask too many questions.
MALE CHORUS. Questions. The child's instinct sup-
   pressed in the adult.
MALE CHORUS. For the sake of order, peace.
MALE CHORUS. But at what price?
MALE CHORUS. I wouldn't want to live in a world that's
   always shifting. Questions are like earthquakes. If
   you're lucky, it's just a rumble.
FIRST SOLDIER. Why don't we ask Tereus if we can go
   home? I want to see my girl.
SECOND SOLDIER. He wants to see his wife.
FIRST SOLDIER. How do you know?
SECOND SOLDIER. He would, wouldn't he?
FIRST SOLDIER. Then why are we here?
SECOND SOLDIER. Ask him.
FIRST SOLDIER. Why don't you?
MALE CHORUS. More days pass. We wait.

FIRST SOLDIER. Why don't we talk to him together?
  Respectful, friendly.
SECOND SOLDIER. And say what?
FIRST SOLDIER. Ask him if he's had any news of home.
  Tell him how nice it is. And spring's coming.
SECOND SOLDIER. I'd leave out the bit about spring.
FIRST SOLDIER. Why?
SECOND SOLDIER. Ready?
  (Pause.)
  Not today. He's worried.
FIRST SOLDIER. What about me?
SECOND SOLDIER. You're not a king. His worry is big-
  ger than yours.
FIRST SOLDIER. Why?
SECOND SOLDIER. It's more interesting.
MALE CHORUS. Days.
MALE CHORUS. Days.
SECOND SOLDIER. Tereus?
TEREUS. Yes.
SECOND SOLDIER. He wants to speak to you.
TEREUS. Speak.
FIRST SOLDIER. Speak.
SECOND SOLDIER. Euh.
  (Pause. TEREUS turns away.)
FIRST SOLDIER. Why are we here?
SECOND SOLDIER. What are we waiting for?
FIRST SOLDIER. Why aren't we going home?
SECOND SOLDIER. Why haven't any messengers been
  sent to tell everyone we're safe?
FIRST SOLDIER. We want to go home.
SECOND SOLDIER. We've had enough.
  (Pause.)
TEREUS. I have my reasons.

MALE CHORUS. An old phrase, but it buys time. More
days.

FIRST SOLDIER. What reasons?

SECOND SOLDIER. Yes, what reasons?

TEREUS. You must trust me.

(Pause.)

Am I not your leader?

SECOND SOLDIER. Yes, Tereus, but—

TEREUS. My knowledge is greater than yours, that is my
duty, just as yours is to trust me. Think: when you fight
wars with me, you see only part of the battle, the few
enemies you kill, or your own wounds. Sometimes this
seems terrible to you, I know, but later you see the vic-
tory and the glory of your country. That glory, fame, I
have seen all along.

SECOND SOLDIER. Yes, Tereus, but—

FIRST SOLDIER. Where's the enemy?

TEREUS. I have information.

MALE CHORUS. More days.

SECOND SOLDIER. Why do we have to wait so long?

FIRST SOLDIER. For what?

SECOND SOLDIER. It's this waiting makes me afraid.
I'd rather something happened, anything.

TEREUS. I know this is difficult for you. *(Pause.)* It's
difficult for me. *(Pause.)* You're experienced soldiers,
responsible citizens, I trust you not to risk the safety
and honour of your country because you don't understand yet. Trust me and you'll understand all in time.

MALE CHORUS. In time...

MALE CHORUS. What hasn't been said and done in the
name of the future? A future always in someone else's
hands. We waited, without the pain of responsibility for
that promised time, the good times. We asked no more

questions and at night, we slept soundly, and did not see:

SCENE ELEVEN

PHILOMELE, NIOBE, TEREUS.

TEREUS. Philomele.

PHILOMELE *(to NIOBE)*. Why does he follow me every-where? Even Procne left me alone sometimes.

NIOBE. Don't make him angry!

PHILOMELE. Let's ignore him.

TEREUS. Philomele.

PHILOMELE. It's spring. Look at these flowers, Niobe, we have them in the woods near Athens. I'll bring some to Procne.

TEREUS. Philomele.

PHILOMELE. And here is some wild thyme, and that is xorta. Procne loves its bitter taste.

TEREUS. Philomele.

PHILOMELE. What is this plant, Niobe? Smell it. It's salty, I've never seen it before. Procne will know.

TEREUS. Philomele!

PHILOMELE. Quiet, brother, you're disturbing the butter-flies. Procne would not like that.

TEREUS. Procne. Procne. Procne is dead.

(Silence.)

There is a mountain not far from the palace. She climbed it with her women to see if she could catch sight of the sea. On a clear day you can look at the sea from there. She climbed to the top, but there was a tall rock and she said she would climb that as well, to see us, to welcome the ship. The women begged her not to, no one would follow her. The rock is slippery and on the other side drops straight into the river below. She climbed, climbed higher to welcome her sister and stood there, waving, safe, the women thought. But then she seemed to grow dizzy, she cried out and suddenly fell, down the rock, down the cliff, into the river swollen now because of the winter rains. They are still looking for her body, it was carried with the torrent. Perhaps better not to find it.

NIOBE. Yes, better. Never look at a battered body, it is worse than the death that came to it.

TEREUS. Mourn, Philomele, mourn with me. She was my wife.

PHILOMELE. Procne.

TEREUS. Procne.

NIOBE. Procne.

(PHILOMELE begins to cry and scream. TEREUS takes her in his arms.)

TEREUS. Sister, beloved sister. My sister.

PHILOMELE. Procne. No! I want to see her body!

CHORUS. Nor did we see, still sleeping:

SCENE TWELVE

PHILOMELE, the CAPTAIN, NIOBE.

PHILOMELE. How long have we been in this place forsaken by the gods, Captain?

CAPTAIN. Almost a full month, Philomele.

PHILOMELE. Why?

(Pause.)

I can't mourn my sister here. Let me at least remember her where she lived all those years. Why do we wait and wait, for what?

CAPTAIN. There may be trouble. Tereus keeps these things to himself.

PHILOMELE. And you, Captain, where will you go?

CAPTAIN. I'm waiting for orders.

PHILOMELE. South?

CAPTAIN. Perhaps.

PHILOMELE. You won't say, you've been asked not to say, why?

CAPTAIN. You ask too many questions, Philomele.

PHILOMELE. And you ask none, why?

(Pause.)

Do you love the sea?

CAPTAIN. Sometimes.

PHILOMELE. I used to watch you at night, standing on your deck, an immense solitude around you. You seemed a king of elements, ordering the wind.

CAPTAIN. No, you guess the wind, you order the sails. The winds have names, they're godlike, man obeys.

PHILOMELE. I never understood obedience, Captain philosophical.

CAPTAIN. You're a woman.

PHILOMELE. Does that make me lawless? Do you have a wife?

CAPTAIN. No, no.

PHILOMELE. Why not?

NIOBE *(muttering)*. Girl without shame. And after a captain when she could have a king.

PHILOMELE. Take me with you.

CAPTAIN. Take you, Where?

PHILOMELE. On the sea. South...Wherever...

CAPTAIN. You're laughing at me, Philomele. Tereus...

PHILOMELE. Frightens me. Since Procne's accident. Perhaps before. His eyes wander, have you noticed? In Athens the philosophers used to talk about wandering eyes. I forget exactly what they said, but it was not good. Yes, the eyes are the windows of the soul—Tereus has a nervous soul.

CAPTAIN. You shouldn't speak like that. Not to me. My job is to obey him.

PHILOMELE. Again! What about your obedience to the elements, and desire, isn't that a god too?

CAPTAIN. Philomele...

PHILOMELE. You touched my hand on the ship once, by mistake, and once I fell against you, a wave, you blushed, I saw it, fear, desire, they're the same, I'm not a child. Touch my hand again: prove you feel nothing.
(She holds out her hand. The CAPTAIN hesitates and touches it.)
So—I was right. Take me with you.

CAPTAIN. We will ask Tereus.

PHILOMELE. We will ask the gods within us. Love...

CAPTAIN. ...your power...

PHILOMELE. Not mine...Between us, above us.

(PHILOMELE takes the CAPTAIN's hand and puts it on her breast. TEREUS enters.)

TEREUS. Traitor! Traitor! Traitor!
(He kills the CAPTAIN.)
A young girl, defenceless.
I'll cut off your genitals.

Go to the underworld with your shame around your
neck.
(Pause.)
Be more careful, Philomele.
MALE CHORUS *(carrying the body off)*. We saw noth-
ing.

SCENE THIRTEEN

Moonlight. The beach. PHILOMELE.

PHILOMELE. Catch the moonlight with your hands. Tread
the moonlight with your toes, phosphorescence, phos-
phorescence, come to me, come to me, tell me the se-
crets of the wine-dark sea.
(Pause.)
I am so lonely.
(Pause.)
Procne, come to me.
(Pause. She waits.)
Procne, Procne, sister. Help me.
Catch the lather of the moonlight. Spirits, talk to me.
Oh, you gods, help me.

(TEREUS enters. PHILOMELE senses this.)

PHILOMELE *(softly)*. Phosphorescence, phosphorescence,
tell me the secrets of the wine-dark sea...
TEREUS *(softly)*. Philomele, what are you doing?
PHILOMELE. Catching the lather of the sea. Moonlight,
moonlight.

TEREUS. I only wish you well...

PHILOMELE. Let me bury my sister.

TEREUS. I told you, we never found the body.

PHILOMELE. Take me to the gorge, I will find it.

TEREUS. Nothing left now, weeks—

PHILOMELE. I will find the bones.

TEREUS. Washed by the river.

PHILOMELE. Let me stand in the river.

TEREUS. It's dangerous.

PHILOMELE. I don't want to stay here.

TEREUS. You have everything you want, you loved the spot when we first came.

PHILOMELE. Then...

Tereus, I want to see my sister's home, I want to speak to the women who were with her, I want to know the last words she said, please, please take me there. Why are we here? What is the point of talking if you won't answer that question?

(Silence. PHILOMELE turns away.)

Moonlight, moonlight ...

TEREUS. Philomele, listen to me.

PHILOMELE. Light the shells, light the stones, light the dust of old men's bones...

TEREUS. Philomele!

PHILOMELE. Catch the lather of the sea...

TEREUS. Do you remember that day in the theatre in Athens? The play?

PHILOMELE. Evanescence, evanescence...

TEREUS. Philomele, I am telling you.

(Pause.)

I love you.

PHILOMELE. I love you too, brother Tereus, you are my sister's husband.

TEREUS. No, no. The play. I am Phaedra. *(Pause.)* I love you.

(Silence.)

PHILOMELE. It is against the law.

TEREUS. My wife is dead.

PHILOMELE. It is still against the law.

TEREUS. The power of the god is above the law. It began then, in the theatre, the chorus told me. I saw the god and I loved you.

PHILOMELE. Tereus.

(Pause.)

I do not love you.

I do not want you.

I want to go back to Athens.

TEREUS. Who can resist the gods? Those are your words, Philomele. They convinced me, your words.

PHILOMELE. Oh, my careless tongue. Procne always said—my wandering tongue. But, Tereus, it was the theatre, it was hot, come back to Athens with me. My parents—Tereus, please, let me go back to Athens.

TEREUS. The god is implacable.

PHILOMELE. You are a king, you are a widower. This is—frivolous.

TEREUS. You call this frivolous.

(He seizes her.)

PHILOMELE. Treachery.

TEREUS. Love me.

PHILOMELE. No.

TEREUS. Then my love will be for both. I will love you and love myself for you. Philomele, I will have you.

PHILOMELE. Tereus. Wait.

TEREUS. The god is out.

PHILOMELE. Let me mourn.

TEREUS. Your darkness and your sadness make you all the more beautiful.

PHILOMELE. I have to consent.

TEREUS. It would be better, but no, you do not have to. Does the god ask permission?

PHILOMELE. Help. Help me. Someone. Niobe!

TEREUS. So, you are afraid. I know fear well. Fear is consent. You see the god and you accept.

PHILOMELE. Niobe!

TEREUS. I will have you in your fear. Trembling limbs to my fire.

(TEREUS grabs PHILOMELE and leads her OFF. NIOBE appears.)

NIOBE. So it's happened. I've seen it coming for weeks. I could have warned her, but what's the point? Nowhere to go. It was already as good as done. I know these things. She should have consented. Easier that way. Now it will be all pain. Well I know. We fought Athens. Foolish of a small island but we were proud. The men—dead. All of them. And us. Well—we wished ourselves dead then, but now I know it's better to live. Life is sweet. You bend your head. It's still sweet. You bend it even more. Power is something you can't resist. That I know. My island bowed its head. I came to Athens. Oh dear, oh dear, she shouldn't scream like that. It only makes it worse. Too tense. More brutal. Well I know. She'll accept it in the end. Have to. We do. And then. When she's like me she'll wish it could happen again. I wouldn't mind a soldier. They don't look at me now. All my life I was afraid of them and then one day they stop looking and it's even more frightening. Be-

cause what makes you invisible is death coming qui-
etly. Makes you pale, then unseen. First, no one turns,
then you're not there. Nobody comes to my island any
more. It's dead too. Countries are like women. It's
when they're fresh they're wanted. Why did the Athenians want our island? I don't know. We only had a few
lemon trees. Now the trees are withered. Nobody looks
at them. There. It's finished now. A cool cloth. On her
cheeks first. That's where it hurts most. The shame.
Then we'll do the rest. I know all about it. It's the
lemon trees I miss, not all of those dead men. Funny,
isn't it? I think of the lemon trees.

SCENE FOURTEEN

*The palace of Tereus. PROCNE and the FEMALE
CHORUS.*

PROCNE. If he is dead then I want to see his body and if
he is alive then I want to see him. That is logical. Iris,
come here. Closer. There.
(Pause.)
Iris, I have seen you look at me with some kindness.
You could be my friend, possibly? What is a friend? A
friend tells the truth. Will you be my friend? No, don't
turn away, I won't impose the whole burden of this
friendship. One gesture, one gift. One question. Will
you be my friend to the tune of one question? Ah, you
don't say no. Iris, answer me. Is Tereus dead?
(Pause.)

Iris, please, pity. One yes, one no. Small words and yet can turn the world inside out.

(Pause.)

I have learned patience. It is the rain.

(Pause.)

The inexorable weight of a grey sky. I can wait.

(Silence.)

It's only one word.

Very well, don't. And when I kill myself, it will be for you to bring news of my death, Iris. You don't believe me? Athenians don't kill themselves. But I can be Thracian too. I have been here long enough. Go now.

IRIS. No.

PROCNE. He is not dead.

IRIS. No.

PROCNE. But then, why?

(Pause.)

Yes, my promise. *(Pause.)* Thank you. My sister? No, of course, another question. If there is one, might there not be two? *(She addresses the WOMEN.)* My husband is not dead. Who will tell me where he is? Why? You have husbands among his men. Don't you ask yourselves questions? What sirens have entangled them in what melodies? Is that it? But no, he is not dead, so he is not drowned. Turned into a wild beast by the power of a witch, is that it? You've heard barking in the forest and recognized your husbands? Don't dare say, the shame of it; my husband is a dog. All fleas, wagging tail and the irrational bite, well, is that it? Weeks, weeks and no one speaks to me.

(Pause.)

Even a rumour would do.

Where are your men?

Where is mine?
Where is Tereus?

(TEREUS and the MALE CHORUS enter.)

TEREUS. Here.
   (Pause.)
   A delay.
PROCNE *(very still).* A delay.
   (Pause.)
   There's blood on your hands.
TEREUS. A wild beast. Or a god in disguise. Unname-
   able.
PROCNE. My sister?
TEREUS *(after a brief pause).* Not here.
PROCNE. No. *(Pause.)* Drowned?
   (Pause.)
TEREUS. But I am here.
PROCNE. Yes.
   (She opens her arms. The MALE CHORUS comes for-
   ward, hiding TEREUS and PROCNE.)
MALE CHORUS. Home at last.
MALE CHORUS. We said nothing.
MALE CHORUS. It was better that way.

SCENE FIFTEEN

PHILOMELE, NIOBE. PHILOMELE is being washed
by NIOBE, her legs spread out around a basin. Her
head is down.

NIOBE. There. Nothing left. It's a weak liquid, it drops out quickly. Not like resin.

PHILOMELE. I can still smell it. Wash me.

NIOBE. It's your own smell, there's nothing left.

PHILOMELE. It's the smell of violence. Wash me.

NIOBE. It's the smell of fear.

PHILOMELE. Wash me.

NIOBE. Some women get to like the smell. I never did. Too much like fishing boats. I like the smell of pines.

PHILOMELE. I want to die. Wash me.

NIOBE. You will, when it's time. In the meantime, get him to provide for you. They don't like us so much afterwards, you know. Now he might still feel something. We must eat. Smile. Beg.

PHILOMELE. Beg? Was it my fault?

NIOBE. I don't ask questions. Get some coins if you can.

PHILOMELE. Goddesses, where were you?

NIOBE. Stop worrying about the gods and think of us. Don't make him angry. He might still be interested. That would be excellent.

PHILOMELE. You. You are worse than him.

(She pours the dirty water over NIOBE.)

Filth. Here. Drink his excretions.

NIOBE. Don't be so mighty, Philomele. You're nothing now. Another victim. Grovel. Like the rest of us.

PHILOMELE. No.

NIOBE. Be careful. Worse things can happen. Keep low. Believe me. I know. Keep silent.

PHILOMELE. Never.

NIOBE. Here's the King. Hold back your tongue, Philomele.

(TEREUS enters.)

TEREUS. Now I wish you didn't exist.

(Pause.)

PHILOMELE. When will you explain, Tereus?

TEREUS. Explain?

PHILOMELE. Why? The cause? I want to understand.

TEREUS. I don't know what to do with you...

PHILOMELE. Me...

(Pause.)

I was the cause, wasn't I? Was I? I said something. What did I do?

(Pause.)

Something in my walk? If I had sung a different song? My hair up, my hair down? It was the beach. I ought not to have been there. I ought not to have been anywhere. I ought not to have been...at all...then there would be no cause. Is that it? Answer.

TEREUS. What?

PHILOMELE. My body bleeding, my spirit ripped open, and I am the cause? No, this cannot be right, why would I cause my own pain? That isn't reasonable. What was it then, tell me, Tereus, if I was not the cause?

(Pause.)

You must know, it was your act, you must know, tell me, why, say.

(Pause.)

It was your act. It was you. I caused nothing.

(Short pause.)

And Procne is not dead. I can smell her on you.

(Pause.)

You. You lied. And you.

What did you tell your wife, my sister, Procne, what did you tell her? Did you tell her you violated her sister, the sister she gave into your trust? Did you tell her what a coward you are and that you could not, cannot bear to look at me? Did you tell her that despite my fear, your violence, when I saw you in your nakedness I couldn't help laughing because you were so shriveled, so ridiculous and it is not the way it is on the statues? Did you tell her you cut me because you yourself had no strength? Did you tell her I pitied her for having in her bed a man who could screech such quick and ugly pleasure, a man of jelly beneath his hard skin, did you tell her that?

(Pause.)

And once I envied her happiness with her northern hero. The leader of men. Take the sword out of your hand, you fold into a cloth. Have they ever looked at you, your soldiers, your subjects.

TEREUS. That's enough.

PHILOMELE. There's nothing inside you. You're only full when you're filled with violence. And they obey you? Look up to you? Have the men and women of Thrace seen you naked? Shall I tell them? Yes, I will talk.

TEREUS. Quiet, woman.

PHILOMELE. You call this man your king, men and women of Thrace, this scarecrow dribbling embarrassed lust, that is what I will say to them, you revere him, but have you looked at him? No? You're too awed, he wears his cloak of might and virility with such ease you won't look beneath. When he murdered a virtuous captain because a woman could love that captain, that was bravery, you say. And if, women of Thrace, he wants to force himself on you, trying to stretch his puny manhood to your intimacies, you call that high spirits? And you soldiers, you'll follow into a battle a man who lies, a man of tiny spirit and shriveled courage? Wouldn't you prefer someone with truth and goodness, self-control and reason? Let my sister rule in his place.

TEREUS. I said that was enough.

PHILOMELE. No, I will say more. They will all know what you are.

TEREUS. I warn you.

PHILOMELE. Men and women of Thrace, come and listen to the truth about this man—

TEREUS. I will keep you quiet.

PHILOMELE. Never, as long as I have the words to expose you. The truth, men and women of Thrace, the truth—

(TEREUS cuts out PHILOMELE's tongue.)

SCENE SIXTEEN

PHILOMELE crouched in a pool of blood. NIOBE.

NIOBE. Now truly I pity Philomele. She has lost her words, all of them. Now she is silent. For good. Of course, he could have killed her, that is the usual way of keeping people silent. But that might have made others talk. The silence of the dead can turn into a wild chorus. But the one alive who cannot speak, that one has truly lost all power. There. I don't know what she wants. I don't know what she feels. Perhaps she likes being silent. No responsibility.

(PHILOMELE seizes her, tries to express something.)

I don't know what she wants. She can no longer command me. What good is a servant without orders? I will go. I don't know what she wants.

(TEREUS enters. PHILOMELE stands still. Silence.)

TEREUS. You should have kept quiet.
(Pause.)
I did what I had to.
(Pause.)
You threatened the order of my rule.
(Pause.)
How could I allow rebellion? I had to keep you quiet. I am not sorry. Except for your pain. But it was you or me.
(Long pause.)
You are more beautiful now in your silence. I could love you. You should have allowed the god to have his way. You should have kept quiet. I was the stronger. And my desire. Niobe, you will look after her. This to ease the pain. *(He gives NIOBE money, then goes to PHILOMELE.)* Why weren't you more careful? Let me kiss those bruised lips. You are mine. My sweet, my songless, my caged bird.
(He kisses her. She is still.)

SCENE SEVENTEEN

Tereus's palace. PHILOMELE, ITYS, TEREUS.

PROCNE. I wouldn't want to be young again. Time flows so gently as you get older. It used to feel broken by rocks. Five years since my sister died. Tomorrow. I will light a candle towards the sea, as I do every year. But the pain flickers now, almost out. Will you come with me this time, Tereus?

TEREUS. No.

PROCNE. I used to be angry that you would not mourn my sister. Why should you mourn her? You hardly knew her. Your aunt, Itys. You would have liked her. She was full of laughter.

ITYS. I have uncles. They're strong.

PROCNE. She could speak with the philosophers. She was bold and quick.

ITYS. What's a philosopher?

PROCNE. A man who loves wisdom.

ITYS. What is wisdom?

PROCNE. It brings peace.

ITYS. I don't like peace. I like war.

PROCNE. Why?

ITYS. So I can be brave. I want to be a great captain. Lead thousands into battle. Like Mars.

PROCNE. Mars is a god.

ITYS. What is a god?

PROCNE. Like us. But doesn't die.

ITYS. Why can't I be a god?

PROCNE. You have to be born one.

TERFUS. But you'll be a king, Itys. That's almost as good.

PROCNE. A wise king, like your father.

ITYS (*turning round with his spear in hand*). I'll fight this way. I'll fight that way. I'll fight this way. I'll fight this way.

(*He runs out.*)

PROCNE. I am happy, as there was to be only one, that we have a son.

(Pause.)

Aren't you?

TEREUS. Yes.

PROCNE. You're quiet.

(Pause.)

Over the years you have become quiet. I used to be afraid of you, did you know? But we shall grow old in peace. I wish more people came to visit this country. Then we could show our hospitality. No one comes here. Why?

(Silence.)

And if a god came to visit, he would find us sitting here, content, and perhaps turn us into two trees as a reward, like Baucis and Philemon. Would you like that?

TEREUS. Not yet.

PROCNE. Ha. I love to see you smile.

(Pause.)

And tomorrow is the feast of Bacchus. I will go out this time. I will go out with the women of this country. You see how I become Thracian.

(Pause.)

You're going? Of course, you must. The evening is soft, look, stars too. We do not have many evenings together. I was frightened of your evenings when we were first married. That is why I sent you to Athens for my sister. I am a woman now. I can take pleasure in my husband.

(She approaches TEREUS, but he puts her away from him and leaves. When he is gone, she holds the bottom of her stomach.)

Desire. Now. So late.

Oh, you gods, you are cruel.

Or, perhaps, only drunk.

(She begins to dress as a Bacchae as does the FEMALE CHORUS. Music.)

SCENE EIGHTEEN

Music. The stage fills with BACCHAE. It's a procession, with a huge doll-like figure of the god in a dress. Mostly women, but men dressed as women also follow the procession. Drums and flutes. Chaos. NIOBE comes on, leading PHILOMELE who carries two huge dolls. Behind her, the SERVANT carries a third doll.

NIOBE. No place safe from the Bacchae. They run the city and the woods, flit along the beach, no crevasse free from the light of their torches. Miles and miles of a drunken chain. These people are savages. Look at their women. You never see them and when you do, breasts hanging out, flutes to their mouths. In my village, they'd be stoned. Out of the way, you, out of the way.

SERVANT. We could move faster without those big dolls, Niobe.

NIOBE. She wouldn't go without them. Years she's been sewing, making them, painting faces. Look. Childlike pastime for her, what can I say? It's kept her still. And she's quiet anyway. Tereus said, get her out, quickly, into the city. She'll be lost there. Another madwoman, no one will notice. Could have cut off her tongue in frenzied singing to the gods. Strange things happen on these nights, I have heard.

SERVANT. Very strange, Niobe. But she was better in the hut.

NIOBE. No. It gives her a little outing. She's only seen us
and the King for five years.

SERVANT. He doesn't come much any more.

NIOBE. No. They all dream of silence, but then it bores
them.

SERVANT. Who is she, Niobe?

NIOBE. No one. No name. Nothing. A king's fancy. No
more.

SERVANT. I feel pity for her, I don't know why.

NIOBE. Look, some acrobats. The idiot will like it. Look.
Look. See the acrobats. Now that's like my village. Except I believe they're women. Shame on them. But still,
no harm in watching.

*(NIOBE thrusts PHILOMELE to the front of a circle,
watching. A CROWD gathers around. The ACROBATS
perform. Finish. As they melt back into the CROWD,
the empty space remains and PHILOMELE throws the
dolls into the circle. NIOBE grabs one of them and tries
to grab PHILOMELE, but she is behind the second
doll. Since the dolls are huge, the struggle seems to be
between the two dolls. One is male, one is female and
the male one has a king's crown.)*

NIOBE. A mad girl, a mad girl. Help me.

*(But the CROWD applauds, makes a wider circle and
waits in silence. The rape is re-enacted in a gross and
comic way, partly because of NIOBE's resistance and
attempt to catch PHILOMELE. PHILOMELE does most
of the work with both dolls. The CROWD laughs. PHIL-
OMELE then stages a very brutal illustration of the cut-
ting of the female doll's tongue. Blood cloth on the*

floor. The CROWD is very silent. NIOBE still. Then the
SERVANT comes inside the circle, holding the third
doll, a queen. At that moment, PROCNE also appears
in the front of the CROWD's circle. She has been watch-
ing. The Procne doll weeps. The two female dolls em-
brace. PROCNE approaches PHILOMELE, looks at her
and takes her away. The dolls are picked up by the
CROWD and they move OFF, enacting other brutal
scenes. A bare stage for a second. Then PROCNE and
PHILOMELE appear, PROCNE holding on to PHIL-
OMELE, almost dragging her. Then she lets go. PHIL-
OMELE stands still. PROCNE circles her, touches her.
Sound of music very distant. Then a long silence. The
SISTERS look at each other.)

PROCNE. How can I know that was the truth?
(Pause.)
You were always wild. How do I know you didn't take
him to your bed?
You could have told him lies about me, cut out your
own tongue in shame. How can I know?
You won't nod, you won't shake your head. I have
never seen him violent. He would not do this.
He had to keep you back from his soldiers. Desire al-
ways burnt in you. Did you play with his sailors? Did
you shame us all? Why should I believe you?
(She shakes PHILOMELE.)
Do something. Make me know you showed the truth.
(Pause.)
There's no shame in your eyes. Why should I believe
you? And perhaps you're not Philomele. A resemblance.
A mockery in this horrible drunken feast. How can I
know?

(Silence.)
But if it is true. My sister.
Open your mouth.
(PHILOMELE opens her mouth, slowly.)
To do this. He would do this.
(Pause.)
's that what the world looks like?
Pause.)
Justice. Philomele, the justice we learned as children, do you remember? Where is it? Come, come with me.
(The BACCHAE give wine to PROCNE and PHILO-MELE.)
Do this.
(PHILOMELE drinks.)
Drink. Oh, we will revel. You, drunken god, help us. Help us.
(They dance OFF with the BACCHAE.)

SCENE NINETEEN

TWO SOLDIERS.

SECOND SOLDIER. Do you want to look in?
FIRST SOLDIER. They'd kill us.
SECOND SOLDIER. That window, there. We could see through the shutters.
FIRST SOLDIER. It's supposed to be a mystery. A woman's mystery. That's what my girl says. Give me a break.
SECOND SOLDIER. You could sit on my shoulders Make sure your girl's behaving.

FIRST SOLDIER. It's all women in there.

SECOND SOLDIER. It's all men in a war.

FIRST SOLDIER. You mean, she—they—no.

SECOND SOLDIER. Have a look.

FIRST SOLDIER. If she—I'll strangle her. So that's what a mystery is. Let me see.

(The FIRST SOLDIER climbs on to the SECOND SOL-DIER's shoulder.)

SECOND SOLDIER. Can you see?

FIRST SOLDIER. Steady.

SECOND SOLDIER. I'm holding your legs. Can you see?

FIRST SOLDIER. Yeah.

SECOND SOLDIER. Well?

FIRST SOLDIER. It's just a lot of women.

SECOND SOLDIER. We know that, stupid. What are they doing?

FIRST SOLDIER. Drinking.

SECOND SOLDIER. And?

FIRST SOLDIER. Oh.

SECOND SOLDIER. What?

FIRST SOLDIER. Oh, you gods.

SECOND SOLDIER. Well? What are they doing? Exactly? What?

FIRST SOLDIER (jumping down, laughing). Nothing.

(He does a dance with the SECOND SOLDIER.)

Dancing. Lots of wine. They've swords and lances.

(ITYS has appeared.)

ITYS. I saw you.

FIRST SOLDIER. No men, no boys on the street. Go home.

ITYS. I saw you looking.

SECOND SOLDIER. That's Itys. Tereus's son. Why
aren't you asleep?

ITYS. I saw you. I'm going to tell my father when he gets
back.

FIRST SOLDIER. Nothing wrong with looking.

ITYS. Mother said no one's to see.
I'll tell her, she'll tell Father. He'll be angry.

SECOND SOLDIER. Don't you want to see?

ITYS. It's not allowed.

SECOND SOLDIER. Aren't you a prince? A king's son?
You let women tell you what is and is not allowed?

ITYS. You shouldn't have looked.

FIRST SOLDIER. It's just women.

SECOND SOLDIER. Why don't you see for yourself? A
king has to be informed.

FIRST SOLDIER. You can sit on my shoulders.

SECOND SOLDIER. Do you know how to sit on some-
body's shoulders? Are you strong enough?

ITYS. Of course I know.

SECOND SOLDIER. You sure? It's difficult.

FIRST SOLDIER. We'll hold you.

SECOND SOLDIER. No, we won't. You have to climb all
by yourself. Like a man. Can you do it?

ITYS. I'll show you.

*(ITYS climbs on the shoulders of the SECOND SOL-
DIER.)*

SECOND SOLDIER. Good. You'll make a soldier yet.
You're too small to reach the window, aren't you?

ITYS. No, I'm not.

SECOND SOLDIER. I think you are.

(ITYS stretches himself to the window and looks. Pause.)

ITYS. Oh.

FIRST SOLDIER. Still dancing, the women?

ITYS. They drink more than my father.

FIRST SOLDIER. But only once a year.

ITYS. There's Mother.

FIRST SOLDIER. What is she doing?

ITYS. Why should I tell you?

SECOND SOLDIER. Quite right, boy. What about the other women?

ITYS. There's one I've never seen before. She looks like a slave. That's my sword. That slave girl. A slave, a girl slave holding my sword. Let me down.

SECOND SOLDIER. Where are you going?

ITYS. To stop them.

FIRST SOLDIER. No.

SECOND SOLDIER. Wait.

(ITYS runs OFF.)

FIRST SOLDIER. Let's go.

SECOND SOLDIER. Let me look. *(He climbs.)* He's there. They've stopped. They're looking at him. It's all right. Procne is holding him. Shows him to the slave girl. He looks up. They've all gone still. He laughs. Oh! *(The SECOND SOLDIER drops down.)*

FIRST SOLDIER. What happened?

SECOND SOLDIER. I'm drunk. I didn't see anything. It didn't happen. The god has touched me with madness. For looking. I'm seeing things. I didn't see anything. Nothing. Nothing. Nothing. Let's go. I didn't see anything. There's Tereus. I don't know anything. I wasn't here.

(They run OFF.)

SCENE TWENTY

The FEMALE CHORUS. PROCNE. PHILOMELE.

HERO. Without the words to demand.

ECHO. Or ask. Plead. Beg for.

JUNE. Without the words to accuse.

HELEN. Without even the words to forgive.

ECHO. The words that help to forget.

HERO. What else was there?

IRIS. To some questions there are no answers. We might ask you now: why does the Vulture eat Prometheus's liver? He brought men intelligence.

ECHO. Why did God want them stupid?

IRIS. We can ask: why did Medea kill her children?

JUNE. Why do countries make war?

HELEN. Why are races exterminated?

HERO. Why do white people cut off the words of blacks?

IRIS. Why do people disappear? The ultimate silence.

ECHO. Not even death recorded.

HELEN. Why are little girls raped and murdered in the car parks of dark cities?

IRIS. What makes the torturer smile?

HERO. We can ask. Words will grope and probably not find. But if you silence the question.

IRIS. Imprison the mind that asks.

ECHO. Cut out its tongue.

HERO. You will have this.

JUNE. We show you a myth.

ECHO. Image. Echo.

HELEN. A child is the future.

HERO. This is what the soldiers did not see.

(ITYS comes running in.)

ITYS. That's my sword. Give me my sword.

PROCNE. Itys.

ITYS. Give me my sword, slave, or I'll kick you. Kill you
all. Cut off your heads. Pick out your eyes.

*(ITYS goes for PHILOMELE. PROCNE holds him.
PHILOMELE still has the sword. PHILOMELE brings
the sword down on his neck. The FEMALE CHORUS
close in front. TEREUS enters.)*

TEREUS. It's daylight at last. The revels are over. Time
to go home.

(Silence. No one moves.)

We're whitewashing the streets. All that wine. Poured
like blood. It's time for you to go home.

(No one moves.)

Stupefied? You should hold your wine better. You've
had your revels. Go on. Stagger home. Procne, tell your
women to go home.

*(PHILOMELE is revealed. Hands bloodied. There is a
silence.)*

I had wanted to say.

PROCNE. Say what, Tereus?

TEREUS. If I could explain.

PROCNE. You have a tongue.

TEREUS. Beyond words.

PROCNE. What?

TEREUS. When I ride my horse into battle, I see where I
am going. But close your eyes for an instant and the
world whirls round. That is what happened. The world
whirled round.

(Pause.)

PROCNE. What kept you silent? Shame?

TEREUS. No.

PROCNE. What?

TEREUS. I can't say. There are no rules.

PROCNE. I obeyed all rules: the rule of parents, the rule of marriage, the rules of my loneliness, you. And now you say. This.

(Long pause.)

TEREUS. I have no other words.

PROCNE. I will help you find them.

(The body of ITYS is revealed.)

If you bend over the stream and search for your reflection, Tereus, this is what it looks like.

TEREUS. Itys. You.

PROCNE. I did nothing. As usual. Let the violence sweep around me.

TEREUS. She—

PROCNE. No. You, Tereus. You bloodied the future. For all of us. We don't want it.

TEREUS. Your own child!

PROCNE. Ours. There are no more rules. There is nothing. The world is bleak. The past a mockery, the future dead. And now I want to die.

TEREUS. I loved her. When I silenced her, it was from love. She didn't want my love. She could only mock, and soon rebel, she was dangerous. I loved my country. I loved my child. You—this.

PROCNE. You wanted something and you took it. That is not love. Look at yourself. That is not love.

TEREUS. How could I know what love was? Who was there to tell me?

PROCNE. Did you ask?

TEREUS. Monsters. Fiends. I will kill you both.
    (*TEREUS takes the sword of ITYS. The FEMALE CHO-
    RUS comes forward.*)
HERO. Tereus pursued the two sisters, but he never
    reached them. The myth has a strange end.
ECHO. No end.
IRIS. Philomele becomes a nightingale.
JUNE. Procne a swallow.
HELEN. And Tereus a hoopoe.
HERO. You might ask, why does the myth end that way?
IRIS. Such a transformation.
ECHO. Metamorphosis.

    (*The BIRDS come on.*)

SCENE TWENTY-ONE

ITYS and the BIRDS.

PHILOMELE (*the NIGHTINGALE*). And now, ask me
    some more questions.
ITYS. I wish you'd sing again.
PHILOMELE. You have to ask me questions first.
    (*Pause.*)
ITYS. Do you like being a nightingale?
PHILOMELE. I like the nights and my voice in the night.
    I like the spring. Otherwise, no, not much, I never liked
    birds, but we were all so angry the bloodshed would
    have gone on forever. So it was better to become a
    nightingale. You see the world differently.

ITYS. Do you like being a nightingale more than being Philomele?

PHILOMELE. Before or after I was silenced?

ITYS. I don't know. Both.

PHILOMELE. I always felt a shadow hanging over me. I asked too many questions.

ITYS. You want me to ask questions.

PHILOMELE. Yes.

ITYS. Will you sing some more?

PHILOMELE. Later.

ITYS. Why doesn't Procne sing?

PHILOMELE. Because she was turned into a swallow and swallows don't sing.

ITYS. Why not?

PHILOMELE. Different job.

ITYS. Oh.

   (Pause.)

   I like it when you sing.

PHILOMELE. Do you understand why it was wrong of Tereus to cut out my tongue?

ITYS. It hurt.

PHILOMELE. Yes, but why was it wrong?

ITYS *(bored)*. I don't know. Why was it wrong?

PHILOMELE. It was wrong because—

ITYS. What does wrong mean?

PHILOMELE. It is what isn't right.

ITYS. What is right?

   (The NIGHTINGALE sings.)

   Didn't you want me to ask questions.

   (Fade.)

END

DIRECTOR'S NOTES

DIRECTOR'S NOTES